CONTEMPORARY'S
Reading
Basics

Introductory Reader

Mc Graw Hill **Wright Group**

Wright Group

ISBN: 0-8092-0666-8

Send all inquiries to:
Wright Group/McGraw-Hill
130 E. Randolph, Suite 400
Chicago, IL 60601
Manufactured in the United States of America.

7 8 9 RRD 12 11

The *McGraw-Hill* Companies

Table of Contents

To the Reader

If reading has never been easy for you,
Contemporary's *Reading Basics* will help. Each
selection in this reader will let you practice
reading. The article or story will grab your
interest and keep you reading to the end. When
you finish reading, you will answer questions to

- check your understanding of the story
- apply reading skills to help your
  understanding of the story

You may answer these questions alone or
with your classmates. You might write the
answers or you might use the questions to
have a discussion. Suggested answers to the
questions are at the back of this book.

Your teacher may ask you to read a
selection after a lesson in the workbook that
ends with a Read On note. Or you may read
these selections any time you wish.

Reading Basics will build your confidence in
your ability to read by letting you practice on
short, interesting stories.

A Home in the North

Why is a snow house the right kind of house for the Arctic?

1 It is 50 degrees below zero. You are dressed all in fur, but the wind is in your face. Now your skin stings. You know that you are getting frostbite on your nose. Your dogs are pulling the sled well. You can ride on the sled if you want. But when you get cold, you run beside it.

2 You have been traveling across the flat land of the Arctic [Ark'•tik] for six days. All around you is nothing but ice and snow. You are tired. The dogs are tired.

3 Suddenly your dogs begin to bark. In the distance, more dogs are barking. You can't see anything but more ice and snow. But you know you are almost home.

4   The dogs run even faster. They run toward three big bumps in the snow. Now your family is crawling out of the bumps to meet you. You have come home to your snow house.

Building a Shelter *muy grande.*

5   The Arctic is a huge place with few people in it. *sius* It is flat, and no trees can grow there. It is bitterly cold in the winter. The wind blows so hard that it feels even colder. The snow house works well in this land.

6   The Eskimo [Es'•kih•moh] people use the word *igloo* [ihg'•loo] to mean any kind of house. A snow house is called an *igluivigag* [ihg•loo'•ee•vih•gahg]. In the central part of the Arctic, Eskimo families built snow houses to live in for the winter. In other parts, Eskimos made snow houses only when they were traveling. The rest of the winter they lived in houses made from sod and stones. In the summer, they made tents out of animal skins.

7   A snow house was made out of snow that had been packed hard by the wind. An Eskimo would use a long snow knife made out of bone to cut blocks of the hard snow. The blocks were about three feet long and a foot and a half wide. The blocks were only four to six inches thick. Even though the Arctic is very cold, there is not

much snow. Cold air is very dry—too dry for snow. So blocks could not be very thick.

8 The blocks were cut out of the place where the snow house would be built. This way the floor was sunk down into the snow, out of the wind. The blocks were piled up in a circle. For each layer, they were placed closer and closer in, until they met in the middle for a domed roof.

9 More blocks were cut from a trench leading out from the dome. With the blocks covering it, this would be a sunken tunnel. The tunnel led up to the snow house, keeping the wind out. Sometimes a wider space in the tunnel would be built as a storeroom.

10 A snow house could be made very quickly. Two men could build one in an hour or two. Speed could be important if you were outside with a storm coming!

11 A hole was cut in the roof of the snow house to let the stale air out. Fresh air would come in through the tunnel. The snow house was heated only with stone lamps. These were little bowls filled with burning seal oil. The snow house really wasn't very warm inside, but it felt warmer just to be out of the wind!

12 On one side of the snow house was a platform made of snow. This was covered with animal skins. The family used the platform as a

seat and as a bed at night. They also built racks to hang up cooking pots and wet clothes.

Close Ties

13 The family cooked over the stone lamps. Most of their food was meat, and it was eaten raw. In fact, *Eskimo* is an American Indian word that means "a person who eats raw meat." Raw meat gave the Eskimos the energy needed to live in this cold land.

14   Sometimes the married children of a family would build other snow houses near the first one. All might be connected by one tunnel.

15   In the long winters, when the sun never comes up, the village people might build a big snow house. There they all gathered to play games, tell stories, or sing songs. They enjoyed being together.

Changing Times

16 Now times have changed. Most Eskimos live in modern frame houses. Instead of dog sleds, they use snowmobiles. Instead of hunting and fishing in the cold, they work at jobs indoors. Today about 100,000 Eskimos live in the Arctic. They call themselves the *Inuit* [Ih'•noo•wuht]. This name means "the people." They live in a world caught between the old ways and the new.

Questions

1. How long did it take to build a snow house for Eskimos who traveled?

2. What does the word *Eskimo* mean?

3. How do people in the Arctic live today?

Antonym/Synonym Search

1. Look for antonyms for the following words: *hot, slower, small, summer, wet, long, soft, thin, down, slowly.*

2. Find the sentences that use antonyms to tell about the air in the snow house.

3. Use a pair of antonyms to tell how the way Eskimos live today is different from the way they lived in the past.

4. Look for synonyms for the following words: *weary, start, enormous, arched, fast, uncooked.*

5. Rewrite the first paragraph in "Building a Shelter" substituting synonyms for as many words as you can.

What Is Color?

How do we see color?
To see color, we first must have light.

1 Our world is full of color. Most people can see colors, but animals cannot. They see the world in shades of black and white.

2 To see color, we first must have light. A flower that is bright yellow in the daytime looks gray or black at night.

Roy G. Biv[1]

3 White light contains all the colors of the rainbow. We see rainbows in the sky when it rains while the sun shines. The sun's rays pass through raindrops. Each raindrop is a prism[2] that splits the sun's rays into a rainbow.

---

[1] Roy G. Biv: a way to remember in order the colors of the rainbow—red, orange, yellow, green, blue, indigo, and violet

[2] prism: a transparent object with three sides that bends a light ray into a rainbow of color

4   When a ray of light goes through a prism, it bends the light ray. Blue light is bent more. Red light is bent less. In this way, the prism splits the ray of light and spreads out the colors. The rainbow of colors is called a spectrum [spek'•trum].

How It Works

5 Light has colors in it. But how does this help us see the colors of things around us? Imagine you are looking at a colored picture on the page of a book. Light comes from the sun or from an electric lamp. It hits the colors on the page. Some of the light is reflected. It bounces off the page and into your eyes. The parts of the picture that are red reflect red light into your eyes. The blue parts of the picture reflect blue light. And so on.

6   When light passes into the eye, it goes to the back of the eye to the retina [reht'•nuh]. The retina has two kinds of cells. Some are shaped like tiny rods. The rods respond to light but not to colors. The other cells, called cones, do respond to color. The rods and cones together form an image on the retina. This image is sent to the brain. Then you can see the picture on the page.

7   The rods in the retina respond even to very dim light. This is why we can see the shapes of things even when it is dark. But the cones do

not work in dim light. This is why, in dim light, we can't see color.

Color Families

8 The colors of the spectrum are grouped into three families. These are red, yellow, and blue. They are called primary colors. All other colors are made from them.

9   Every color has an opposite. It's called a complementary [kom•pleh•ment'•uh•ree] color. As an example, yellow is the complementary color to blue. Blue green is the complementary color to red.

10   If we look at one color and then look at a different color, our eyes have to change. Most of the time, we don't even notice. Sometimes, though, we can be surprised.

11   For example, stare at a brightly colored picture for about 30 seconds. Then move your eyes quickly to a blank piece of white paper. You will see an afterimage—an image with the same shape as the original image but different colors. The afterimage will stay on your retina for a few moments because your eyes can't change that fast. Where the picture was yellow, you will see blue. Where the picture was blue green, you will see red. And you will see white where the picture was black.

12   Knowing how we see color takes away some of its mystery, but, luckily, none of its beauty.

Questions

1. How does a prism work?

2. How does light help us see the colors of things around us?

3. Which cells in the retina respond to color?

4. Why can we see shapes of things in dim light but not colors of things?

Using Context Clues

1. Which colors are primary colors?

2. What are complementary colors?

3. What is an afterimage?

hide = verb = esconder, ocultar

Who Wears the Pants?

When did people start wearing pants and why?

1 During the Ice Age, the first people wore only animal hides. Then the earth grew warmer, and the ice melted. Cloth was invented about 10,000 years ago. Men would just wrap a piece of cloth around their middles. This was called a loincloth. Today, men still wear loincloths in countries where it is hot, such as India.

2 People learned to sew cloth into clothes. Men began to wear robes, or tunics [too′•niks]. Then, about 3,000 years ago, a tribe from Persia [Pur′•zhah] made war on other tribes. The Persian men were great horsemen. And they wore pants. It just isn't easy to ride a horse in a skirt!

3 In countries with warm weather, men went on wearing robes. But in colder parts of the

14

world, men wore pants. The Vikings wrapped
ties in a crisscross around their legs on top of
the pants.

Fancy Pants

4 Men did not always wear long pants. Until
about 1800, men wore short pants and stockings
when they dressed up. That way, everyone
could admire their good-looking legs. The men
would look in the mirror to decide which of
their legs was better looking. When they went
to a party, they would stand with that leg in
front of the other. We still tell people to put
their best foot forward.

5 Sometimes men had special pants to wear
just to parties. These pants were very tight. The
men couldn't sit down all evening!

What's Good for the Goose . . .

6 When did women start wearing pants?
Through most of history, men fought in wars.
The sports they played often were warlike, too.
Women stayed at home. At last, around 1850,
women began to be active in sports. But what
could they wear? The style at the time was
long, full skirts that got in the way.

7 A woman named Amelia Bloomer had an
idea. She said women should wear loose pants
that came down to the knee. Everyone laughed

at her. Then the bicycle was invented. Women found that their skirts got caught in the gears. So, by 1890, pants for women were very popular. And they were called bloomers!

8   Women still wore pants only for sports. Then movie stars began wearing pants in films. But it was World War II, in the 1940s, that really got women into pants for good.

9   During the war, it was hard for women to buy stockings. So they wore pants to cover their bare legs. Many women also worked in factories while the men were away at war. Pants just made more sense for that kind of work.

10   Women were still not wearing pants when they dressed up. They could not wear pants to a fancy restaurant. Nor could they wear them to work in a bank or as teachers. But women kept wearing pants. A matching jacket gave pants a more formal look. By the 1970s, people were used to seeing women in pantsuits.

A Choice for All

11   Today no one is surprised at seeing women in pants. Everyone wears them. But people are not used to seeing men in skirts. The men of Scotland sometimes wear skirts called kilts. In Scotland's early days, men did not wear kilts. They wore shirts and pants with crisscross ties on the legs.

12 Poor people in that country wrapped themselves in warm plaid [plad] blankets. Scotland is famous for its plaid wool cloth. A plaid pattern has colored stripes going in two different directions. Rich people, too, wore plaid blankets as they hunted or farmed. In the 1600s, people started to cut the blanket into pieces of cloth. Each piece was two feet wide and six feet long. A belt held the cloth in place.

13 By the 1700s, they folded the cloth into pleats. Men from the Highlands wore these pleated skirts, or kilts, to show which part of Scotland they came from. They wore the kilt with a shirt, jacket, and knee socks. Another piece of plaid cloth was draped over the shoulder. This is what proud men of Scotland still wear on special days. Scottish men wear kilts to show that Scotland is still alive and proud.

Questions

1. Why did men start wearing pants?

2. When did women first wear pants? Why?

3. How did World War II affect what women wore?

4. What is a plaid?

5. Why do men in Scotland wear kilts?

Spelling Word Alert

1. Find the sentences that use the following words: *piece, sew, wear, great, bare, sense, two*. Write a homophone for each.

2. Find a word with a silent letter that names a part of the body. Find another word with a silent letter that tells what you do to a gift before you give it.

3. Find the sentences with the words *admire* and *decide*. Add *-ing* to the words.

Egypt's Wonders

Have you ever wondered why the pyramids were built? Or why the kings of Egypt were made into mummies?

1   What if you were a king? What if you believed that you could live forever if your body were kept safe after you died? What would you do? You'd build a very safe place for your body.

2   That's just what the kings of Egypt did more than 4,000 years ago. Each one had a huge pyramid [peer'•ah•mid] built as a tomb. The body was placed in a secret room inside the pyramid. Two million blocks of stone protected the body.

3   The largest pyramid of all still stands in Egypt next to the Nile River. It was built just for King Khufu [Koo'•foo]. The base is square. It covers enough ground for ten football fields. The pyramid is 481 feet high. It is made of two

million stone blocks. Each block weighs about 2½ tons. But the men who built King Khufu's pyramid, known as the Great Pyramid, had no power tools. Each block was cut and moved into place by hand!

Hard Labor

4   Thousands of men worked year round to cut and smooth the blocks. They used tools made of copper, stone, and wood. Then a work crew of 50,000 farmers was brought in to move the stones.

5   The farmers worked on the pyramid from July to November each year. During this time, their fields were flooded with water from the Nile River. Work gangs of 25 men moved one stone at a time. Their only pay was food and clothing.

6   Most of the blocks were cut near the building site. But some were cut across the river, and others were cut hundreds of miles away. These had to be brought down the Nile River by boat.

7   Workers made the site level. They cut a trench in the rock all the way around the site. The trench was then filled with water. The rest of the site was cut down or filled in to match the level of the water.

8   The work gangs dragged in the big stone blocks. They laid a long row of logs in the sand

so that the blocks would not sink. Each block was placed on a wooden sled. A team of 20 men pulled the sled over the logs. The workers slid the blocks into place. Each block had to fit just right, or the whole pyramid would be weak. The first layer of blocks was done.

9   The workers continued. They built a ramp of stones and mud to drag the blocks up to the next layer.

Sky High

10 The ramp went up and around, layer after layer. In all, the pyramid had more than 120 layers, each smaller than the one before it. The sides were four triangles that came together to one point at the top. This shape made you look high up toward the sky and the sun.

11   At the very top, a huge capstone was put in place. Then white casing stones were placed over the blocks to make the outside of the pyramid smooth. The snug fit of these stones made the pyramid look as if it has been cut from one huge stone.

A Look Inside

12 Deep inside the pyramid, secret rooms were built. The walls were painted with beautiful pictures and writing that told about the king's life. When the king died, his body would rest

in one of these rooms. Other rooms would store his gold, treasures, and the everyday things he might need in the afterlife.

13   Long hallways inside the tomb led to the secret rooms. Painted on these walls, too, were many beautiful pictures. Perhaps, in the afterlife, the king would not need light to see them.

14   What was it like for the workers to walk through these long passages, in the dark and under millions of tons of stone? The work had taken 25 years to finish. Thousands of workers had been killed by the heavy blocks.

Careful Preparation

15   After death, the king's body had to be preserved so that his soul could live forever. First, special workers took out the brain through the nose with small hooks. Then they took out the lungs and stomach through a cut in the left side of the body. They put these into jars to preserve them.

16   Next, the body was dried in salt and then washed. It was wrapped in layers of cloth. Gold and jewels were placed within the wrappings. In the dry air of Egypt, the preserved body, called a "mummy," would keep year after year.

A Long Journey

17 When the mummy was ready, priests carried it into the pyramid. In a long ceremony [seh'•reh•moh•nee], they placed the mummy in the tomb. Besides the king's treasures, the rooms were filled with food, clothing, furniture, and weapons. Even games were placed in these rooms, in case the king became bored. Forever is a long time!

18 Then the hallways were sealed. Workers put the last casing stones into place on the outside of the pyramid. This way, no one would know where the entrance was.

19 But the people did find the entrance to the tomb. Over the years, robbers broke into the pyramids and stole the gold and jewels. Sometimes they destroyed the mummies, too. But the pyramids were built so well that they still stand.

20 Perhaps King Khufu didn't live forever. But his pyramid has kept his name alive for almost 5,000 years.

Questions

1. What were the pyramids built for?

2. Why did the farmers work only from July to November of each year?

3. Why was the king's body preserved?

4. Why did people later want to enter the pyramid?

Noting Details

1. How tall is King Khufu's pyramid?

2. What is another name for King Khufu's pyramid?

3. How did the workers get the big stone blocks up to each layer of the pyramid?

4. How many layers were there in the pyramid?

5. What was on the walls of the secret rooms in the pyramid?

6. What was the last step in preserving the body of the king?

A Good Cup of Coffee

Why do we feel more alert when we drink coffee?

1 What do you drink when you feel tired or when you just want to take a break? Many people like a cup of hot coffee.

2   Coffee comes from beans. They grow on trees with green shiny leaves. Coffee trees grow only where it is warm all year round. They also need lots of rain. Coffee trees grow high in the mountains. The best trees are in South America and Africa.

Where It Comes From

3 Coffee trees grow on plantations. Workers prune the trees so that they stay under 15 feet tall. This makes it easy to pick the beans.

4   The beans start as pretty, white flowers. When the flowers drop, bunches of green coffee berries start to grow. Each berry has two beans in it. The berries turn red as they ripen. It takes from 6 to 14 months for them to get ripe. On some plantations, all the berries are picked at once. But for the very best coffee, workers pick only the ripe berries.

Green Gold

5 Picking the berries is the first step. The berries go through many more steps before they can be made into coffee. The berries are spread out in the sun to dry. Next, workers rake them to be sure they all get dry. Then they put the berries into a machine to rub off the outer hulls. The beans remain, but they are still green. The workers call them green gold.

6   The coffee beans are shipped to other countries. They still are not ready to be made into coffee. They are roasted until they turn brown. Then the beans are put through big rollers that grind them. Most coffee that we drink does not come from just one kind of bean. It is made from a blend of beans from different kinds of trees. Some people work as trained tasters. They sip the coffees to see how they should be blended. Then the coffee is packed

in airtight containers. It is finally ready to go to the stores.

Look Alive!

7 Why do people drink coffee when they are tired? Coffee contains a drug called caffeine [ka•feen']. By itself, caffeine is white, like sugar. Caffeine stimulates the body's nervous system. This makes a person feel more alert. It also helps the brain work a little faster.

8 Caffeine also stimulates the heart and the stomach. This is bad for some people. It keeps some coffee drinkers awake at night. For these reasons, many people drink decaffeinated [dee•kaf'•fi•nay•tud] coffee. This brew has had much of the caffeine removed.

9 While they are still green, coffee beans are treated with a chemical. This chemical joins itself to the caffeine. Then the chemical is steamed out, taking the caffeine with it. Like regular coffee beans, these beans are dried, roasted, and ground. Both kinds of beans can also be used to make instant coffee.

How It Began

10 We drink billions of cups of coffee each year. People in the United States drink one-third of all the coffee in the world! How did it all start?

Coffee trees first grew in Africa. People there chewed the berries to stay awake. Then they found that they could grind the beans to make a drink. Coffee became very popular. Trees were planted in many other places.

11   There were no coffee trees in North America or South America. Around 1700, a young French soldier brought one tree from a garden in France. He carried it to North America on a sailing ship. It was a long, hard trip. The people on the ship began to run out of drinking water. But the young soldier shared his water with the tree, and he kept it alive. When he got to North America, he planted the tree. Almost all the coffee trees in this part of the world come from that one tree!

A Popular Custom

12 Throughout history, thousands of lively talks about art and politics have taken place in coffeehouses. And they are popular places today for the same reasons. Important decisions have been made over cups of coffee. There are even songs about coffee. Its good taste and smell has placed coffee among the most popular of all hot drinks. Whether taken black, creamed, weak, or strong, it seems that coffee is here to stay.

Questions

1. Where are the best coffee trees in the world?

2. How long does it take for coffee berries to ripen?

3. How is caffeine taken out of coffee?

4. How did coffee first come to North America?

Identifying Sequence

1. What is the first thing that is done to the coffee berries after they have been picked?

2. When are the coffee beans roasted?

3. What is the last thing that is done to the coffee before it is shipped to stores?

The Trail of Tears

What made the Trail of Tears such a tragic event in American history?

1   It was a sad sight. Thousands of men, women, and children trudged across the land. Soldiers forced them on with gun butts. Many fell dead from hunger and cold. The Native American Cherokee people will never forget or forgive this Trail of Tears.

Quiet Lives

2   The Cherokees once lived in the Great Smoky Mountains of Tennessee. For hundreds of years, they lived quiet lives high in the mountains. The Cherokees hunted in the woods and fished in the streams.

3   When white people settled the land, Cherokee life changed. To try to save what land was left, the Cherokees began to live as

the settlers did. Like their white neighbors, they became farmers.

4　In 1828, gold was found in the Smokies. The discovery brought heartbreak to the Cherokee Nation. White men wanted the gold. To get it, they wanted the Cherokees to move away. The settlers also wanted the Cherokee land for farming. They hoped to set up their own farms with fields these Native Americans had cleared.

5　In 1830, the United States government stepped in—to side with the settlers! The government said that the Cherokees would have to relocate. They would have to move west to Oklahoma Territory and set up new farms there.

6　The Cherokees did not want to move away. The Smokies had always been their home. The Cherokees asked President Andrew Jackson to help them, but he said no.

Troops Arrive

7　In 1838, United States troops came to the Smokies. They began to round up the Cherokees. Only 1,000 Cherokee people got away. They hid deep in the mountains. The rest of the Cherokees were caught.

8　Soldiers dragged men from their fields. They pulled women and children from their homes. The troops showed no kindness to the frightened Cherokees. The soldiers shouted at them in English. It was a language many Cherokees did not understand.

9   Soldiers forced the Cherokees into stockades and split up their families. Some children wound up in camps far from their parents. The soldiers did not care. They had orders to move the Cherokee people.

A Long, Hard March

10 When the camps were filled, the long march began. Armed soldiers put the Cherokees into 17 large groups and pushed them west. About 15,000 Cherokees set out.

11   The march was grim from the start. The Cherokees were herded onward like cattle. Some were shoved into wagons. A few rode on horses. Most of the people had to walk. They did not have enough blankets or warm clothes. Many did not even have shoes.

12   Children cried as they waved good-bye to their mountain homes. Men and women also cried. As one Cherokee said,". . . all look[ed] sad like when friends die."

13   Oklahoma was a thousand miles away. To get there, the Cherokees had to tramp through mud and dust. They slogged through rain, sleet, and snow. John Burnett was a soldier on the march. He later wrote about that time. "The

sufferings of the Cherokee[s] were awful," he said. "The trail of the exiles was a trail of death. They had to sleep in the wagons and on the grounds without fire. And I have known as many as 22 of them to die in one night. . . ."

Death on the Trail

14 Some people died from the cold. They shivered and shook but could not get warm. At last, their bodies ran out of heat. Others, too tired to keep going, died from exhaustion [eg•zaus′•chun]. Still others died from disease; they were too weak to fight off sickness.

15 Hunger was always a problem. The marchers had only the food they could carry with them. Their grain sacks got wet and were soon filled with bugs. No one had enough to eat. They all grew weak. Many Cherokees starved to death.

Cruel Treatment

16 The soldiers saw the pain and death they were causing. Yet they kept the groups of Cherokees moving anyway. It was hard for old people to keep up the pace. The heartless soldiers whipped them to make them move faster.

17 Mothers with young children struggled along. Burnett told of one woman with three small children. She set out ". . . with a baby

strapped on her back and leading a child with each hand." As Burnett told it, "the task was too great for that frail mother. . . . She sank and died with her baby on her back and her other two children clinging to her hands."

18   There was no time to give the dead funerals or burial. The soldiers forced the groups to keep moving. Bodies of the dead were thrown into ditches dug along the trail.

19   After about six months, the march ended. The Cherokees had reached Oklahoma. By then, 4,000 people had died. More than one-fourth of those who set out died on the Trail of Tears.

A Different Life

20 The Cherokees looked at their new land. It was not at all like their old home The land was flat, dry, and hot. The Cherokees had to start new lives. But they never forgot the horrors of the long march. They named it the "Trail Where We Cried." Today it is called the Trail of Tears. The trail still marks a sad chapter in United States history.

Questions

1. Where was the Cherokees' original home?

2. Who was the president at the time of the march?

3. What problems did the Cherokees face during the march?

4. What happened to the marchers who died on the way to Oklahoma?

5. About how long did it take the Cherokees to march to Oklahoma?

Recognizing Stated Concepts

1. How did the discovery of gold in the Smoky Mountains affect the Cherokees?

2. How did the United States government settle the dispute between the settlers and the Cherokees?

3. Why was hunger always a problem on the march?

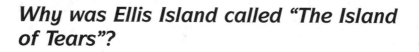

Ellis Island

Why was Ellis Island called "The Island of Tears"?

1 Why does Ellis Island have a special place in American history? Ellis Island was the country's first immigration [im•mih•gray'•shun] port of entry. It lies about a half-mile north of the Statue of Liberty. From 1892 to 1954, about 15 million people came through its gates. Today, more than 100 million Americans have an ancestor who passed through Ellis Island.

2 Most immigrants arrived by ship from Europe. Their life in the old country was hard. It wasn't easy to find work. They were tired of unfair treatment. Some wanted to escape army service. Others had family members who had left for America earlier. Their families' letters had told of jobs and good living conditions.

There was a chance for a better life. Some even believed the streets were paved with gold!

Journey to America

3 Try to imagine a family ready to leave their homeland. They had filled out the necessary forms. Their relatives in the United States had sent tickets and money. Everything they could take was packed. They would need clothing, bedding, and food for the journey.

4 Their ocean voyage could take as long as three weeks. The luckier ones traveled as first class passengers. But many came by way of steerage class. For those people, life on board was full of hardships. They slept and ate in close quarters. But finally, the ship arrived at New York. The people were greeted by a welcome sight: the Statue of Liberty.

5 What was it like when they got off the ship? The travelers were tired but very excited. They wanted to meet their family and see the land of their dreams. But they weren't allowed to enter the city yet. First they boarded a ferry for Ellis Island. What they faced next was not always pleasant.

Island of Tears

6 In the main building, noise surrounded them. There was shouting and pushing. And so

many languages were spoken! Guards called out the numbers of the tags the immigrants wore on their coats. They joined a long, slow-moving line.

7   Papers were checked and questions asked. "What's your name?" "Do you have a job skill?" "Who sent you tickets?" "Can you read and write?" "Do you want to harm the government?"

8   Then came the part feared most: the health station. That's where doctors checked over the newcomers. If the doctors found a heart problem or eye disease, they could send the person back to where he or she came from. Nothing could be worse than that!

9   If one family member failed the health check, what about the rest? Should the whole family go back? Should one parent or an older child go back with the sick person? Such heartbreak is why Ellis Island was often called "The Island of Tears." Only about 250,000 (2 percent) of the immigrants at Ellis Island were deported [dee•por'•ted].

10   What relief for a family who passed through the lines with no problems! Finally, they were able to board another ferry. It would take them to the land of promise. But there was more to do. They had to change the money of their

country into U.S. dollars. Many had to buy train tickets to go on to another city.

11   Not all immigrants came through Ellis Island. Some came through Philadelphia [Fil•a•del'•fee•a], San Francisco, Boston, Galveston, and other ports. But those cities never matched the large numbers that came through New York.

A Closed Door

12 After World War I, some laws changed. The United States let fewer immigrants enter the country. And those who could come were checked before they left the old country. Another rule was that adult immigrants had to take reading and writing tests. The tests were in their own language or in English. If they failed the tests, the people were sent back to their native land. These new rules marked the end of Ellis Island's being a major immigration center.

13   During World Wars I and II, Ellis Island had other uses. The U.S. Army, Navy, and Coast Guard needed the buildings for way stations and a hospital. Ellis Island was also for aliens [ay'•lee•ehns], or people thought to be enemies. The government held them there and then forced them to return to their

native country. At the end of 1954, Ellis Island was closed.

Courage Remembered

14 In 1965, Ellis Island became part of the Statue of Liberty National Monument. Many visitors at the statue wanted to see Ellis Island, too. They had heard stories about it from their grandparents. It opened to the public in 1976. It closed again in 1984 to be restored.

15 Six years later, Ellis Island reopened as a museum and a memorial. Tens of thousands of people have visited. They view films and exhibits. Some exhibits have old photos of the immigrants. Others have items the immigrants brought from their countries. There are displays that visitors can operate. One has a computer people can use to find names of family members. As they walk through the halls, many hope to capture the spirit of their ancestors. And they think about how lucky they are.

Questions

1. About how many Americans have ancestors that came through Ellis Island?

2. Why did people want to come to the United States?

3. What was the immigrants' greatest fear?

4. What is Ellis Island used for today?

Signs and Map Skills

1. Draw pictures of the signs the immigrants might have seen after they arrived on Ellis Island.

2. Use a map to locate the U.S. cities that were the major ports of entry for the immigrants, according to the article. Give the coordinates for each city.

3. Use a map to locate Europe and the body of water that the immigrants crossed to get to Ellis Island.

Building a Budget

Do you know where your money really goes?

1 Does every person need a budget? Before you answer this question, consider a few more. Are you always running out of money? Do you pay your bills late? Will you need to buy a car someday? Will you need more schooling? If you answered "yes" to any of those questions, you probably need a budget.

2   What is a budget? It's a spending plan. The main parts of the plan are income and expenses. The money we earn is income. The things we spend money on are expenses. For a budget to work, expenses cannot be more than income.

Starting Out

3 Before you start a budget, you need to know your net income. That's the amount of money

you actually get. For example, your salary may be $300 a week. But your paycheck is less than that. Items such as taxes and insurance are taken out, or deducted. If you have a paycheck, study it to see what was taken out.

4   Knowing your net income is pretty easy. The hard part is figuring out what your expenses are. It helps to write a list. Put the necessary costs first. List food, rent or mortgage [more'•ghedj] payments, electricity, gas, and telephone. Then add bus or train fare, car payments, clothing costs, and school and book fees. Also add any other expenses.

5   You may find it helpful to list these costs on a chart. Use headings like "Food," "Clothing," "Rent," and "Transportation." You might list movies, concerts, and rental tapes under "Entertainment." What you spend in restaurants can go under "Food" or "Entertainment." List things wherever they make sense to you.

Getting It Together

6 How will you get information about your spending? Some of it will be easy to figure out. Other costs may be harder to gather. You get receipts for most things you buy. Save those receipts. If you have a charge account, the statements can help you. Now is the time to

begin your record keeping. At the end of each day, write down what you have spent.

7   Keep track of your expenses for a month. This will give you a good idea of where the money goes. You may be quite surprised. Eating in restaurants and buying snacks may be costing you a lot. A few items of new clothing might add up to hundreds of dollars. But that doesn't mean you should stop eating out or shopping. It may mean only that you have to spend more carefully.

8   Some expenses, like car insurance, come only once or twice a year. You may want to figure out what it comes to for each month. That will help you plan a monthly budget.

9   Keeping records may sound like a lot of work. It is, but it's time well spent. And it's not a chore you must do forever. Once you see where your money goes, you can control your spending.

Looking Ahead

10 This is a good time to think about the future, too. Perhaps you're planning to buy a car or a house. You may need money for future schooling or vacations. These things are costly. You need to put money away to pay for them.

11   Have you heard the old saying "Save for a rainy day"? It's not really about weather. It's

about being prepared. Something might happen—good or bad—for which you haven't planned. That's a reason to have savings. Try to save some money from each paycheck. Put it in a savings bank or other safe place.

Belt Tightening

12 What if you find that you spend more than you earn? Then you had better look hard at your spending. Look for ways to cut back. Use food expenses as an example. Maybe you can eat in restaurants less often. Maybe you can cook meals from scratch instead of buying prepared foods. Try to become a more careful shopper. Watch for special sales. Perhaps an item costs less one week. Buying enough for a month will save you money.

13   Budgeting isn't easy. It's hard to change your spending habits. But remember, the money you *don't* spend can be put to good use. You can spend it on that "rainy day" and on a wonderful future!

Questions

1. Why is a budget important?

2. What are the two main parts of a budget?

3. How does income differ from net income?

4. What are some ways to figure out how much money you spend every month?

Making Graphs

1. Create a monthly budget for yourself. Write down the necessary costs: food, rent or mortgage, electricity, gas, and telephone. Then add other expenses you have. Subtract these expenses from your total monthly income. Decide if you can spend less on some expenses to save more money.

2. Show your monthly budget on a bar graph. Make bars that show what you spend on rent, food, clothing, transportation, entertainment, and other items.

Armchair Shopping

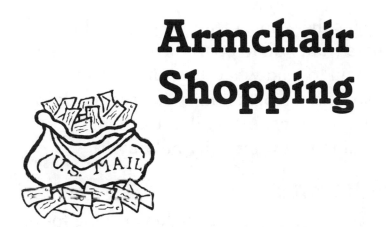

Is the ease of buying through the mail worth the risks?

1 When you got to the mailbox, it's there. Sometimes it's in a plain envelope. Or the envelope may be big and shiny. It may even come as a full-color catalog. The nice term for it is "direct mail." The other term is "junk mail."

Toss or Read?

2 Some people toss all their junk mail right into the trash. Most people, though, don't do that. They pick and choose. They throw out much of this mail after a quick glance. It holds no interest for them. But other pieces look intriguing [in•treeg'•eng]. These are the ones that people open and read.

3   That's the whole idea of direct mail. Direct mailers want you to open their letters. They want you to read what they write and then buy something. Sometimes that seems like a pretty good idea. After all, if the item is something you want, why not buy it?

How Handy!

4 Direct-mail buying has two things going for it. First, it's convenient [kun•veen'•yunt]. You can stay home and be an armchair shopper. All you have to do is write a check and lick a stamp. Or you can make a toll-free call with your credit card in hand.

5   Second, direct-mail firms give you a lot of choices. They offer a wider span of merchandise than stores do. Direct-mail firms that sell clothing or shoes carry all sizes. Many times, local shops don't have the room to store all their goods in every odd size.

The Downside

6 There are also reasons *not* to buy through the mail. Three big problems come to mind. First, you can't inspect what you are buying. That is important when you buy clothing. With good direct-mail companies, this may not be a problem. They show good pictures in their catalogs and describe each item with care.

Still, you can't feel the fabric with your own hands before you buy.

7   Second, costs for shipping and handling can add up. When you buy through the mail, you pay all shipping costs. These fees can sometimes be pretty steep. Some firms add on a charge for what they call insurance. That is a false fee. By law, all mail-order firms must get a product to you in perfect shape. An insurance charge is, in fact, nothing more than a price hike.

8   Third, you have to wait to get what you buy. The law says that a firm must get goods to you within 30 days. But that law does not apply if the seller states a later date in print. A company can then take from five to eight weeks to get an order to you. If the seller doesn't make the deadline stated, you have a choice. You can wait for the order even longer. Or you can get your money back.

9   With good mail-order firms, these are not big problems. They deliver the product quickly, and their goods are top of the line. These firms will also return your money if you don't like the product. Some of the best direct-mail firms are ones that sell clothing, outdoor gear, and hard-to-find tools.

Protect Yourself

10 How can you protect yourself when you buy through the mail? Here are some tips:

11 **1.** Read with care what the catalog says. Photos may look nice, but they can mislead you. If an item sounds too good to be true, it is!

12 **2.** Find out what the company's return policy is. Who pays for shipping costs if you return an item? Many times, *you* will! But you don't need to pay for the company's mistakes. It would be the company's mistake if, for instance, you got a shirt in a size you didn't order. The same is true if an item's color doesn't match the catalog color. Maybe the stitching on an item is poorly done. That is the company's fault. On the other hand, who is at fault if you return an item because you changed your mind?

13 **3.** Know the facts. If you place an order by phone, note the date and time. Write the name of the person who takes your order. Also jot down any order number the phone clerk gives you. Keep the catalog. Mark the pages and circle the items you order.

14 **4.** Protect yourself when you pay for mail-order goods. The best way is to pay by credit card. That way, if something goes wrong, it is easy to cancel your debt. You might pay by check. Most of the time, that's fine. But what if you have a complaint about an item you get? What if the firm goes bankrupt? In both cases, the company can cash your check but not make good on your order. The worst way to pay is to send cash through the mail. Not only do you risk losing the cash—but most direct-mail firms won't take it.

Mountain of Mail

15 How many catalogs do you really want? The more items you order by mail, the more catalogs you will get. The reason is that direct-mail firms sell your name to other firms. You may get catalogs from firms you've never heard of. That's because your name has been sold to those companies.

16   You can put a stop to all of the junk mail. You can write to the Direct Marketing Association [uh•so•see•a'•shun] in New York City. Ask them to take your name off their list. Then, *presto,* no more catalogs—*if* that's what you want.

17   Most people like to get catalogs. They like the convenience of shopping by mail. Maybe you do, too. But use common sense when you buy this way. You can then enjoy the pluses of armchair shopping and avoid most of the minuses.

Questions

1. Why do some people call direct mail "junk mail"?

2. Name two good reasons for buying through the mail.

3. What are the risks of buying through the mail?

4. Why is paying by credit card the best way to buy through the mail?

5. How can you stop junk mail, such as unwanted catalogs?

Using Consumer Materials

1. Identify and write what abbreviations such as *COD, F.O.B., H/C, est., min., lbs., item no., qty.,* and *exp. date* stand for in a direct-mail catalog.

2. Fill out a mail-order form, making sure you have filled in all information. Ask another person to check your order.

3. Figure out the shipping and handling costs for your order. Compare the costs of different shipping options.

The Fabulous Miss Bly

Why would a newspaper reporter want to stay at a home for the mentally ill?

1   In 1890, New York held a parade in honor of Elizabeth Cochrane [Kock'•run]. Was she a movie star? An astronaut [as'•tro•naht]? A visiting princess? No. She was a newspaper reporter. She was about 23 years old. And she had just circled the globe in 72 days.

2   In those days, many young women had hard, dull jobs. Their pay was low. Almost all good jobs went to men. After all, people said, a woman's place is in the home. In 1885, the *Pittsburgh Dispatch* printed an editorial about working women. It said that women could not do a good job outside the home.

Look Out, World!

3 Elizabeth Cochrane read the article. She was young and eager for adventure. The article made her angry. She wrote to the *Dispatch*. Women, she said, could do many jobs well. It was wrong to waste their talents. The paper printed her letter. Then Cochrane asked for a job as a reporter. The editor liked her letter. So he gave her a try.

4 Cochrane wrote under another name. She chose Nellie Bly. "Nellie Bly" is the name of a song by Stephen Foster, an American songwriter who lived in the 1800s.

Travel to Mexico

5 Nellie Bly's first reports told about the hard lives of other working women. She wrote about the slums of Pittsburgh. She wrote about divorce. She got readers excited about her topics.

6 The *Dispatch* saw how popular Bly's work was. So in 1887 the paper sent her to Mexico. For six months, Bly traveled around Mexico. She wrote reports about all that she saw.

7 In those days, few people saw other countries. There were no movies or TV shows about far-off lands. So almost everything in Bly's reports was new to her readers. They were eager to learn about Mexico. Later, Bly

published her reports in a book called *Six Months in Mexico.*

Bly Tells All

8 Soon after Bly came home to Pittsburgh, she moved to New York. She had a new job with a larger paper. She then worked for the *New York World.*

9   Bly's first big topic in New York was insane asylums [uh•sy'•lums]. Most often, the city asylums made little news. People with mental illnesses were just "put away" and forgotten. But how well were patients treated? Bly wanted to find out.

10   Bly knew that visitors are always shown the best things. She wanted to see the worst things, too. So she pretended to be insane. She was sent to a New York asylum as a patient.

11   Inside, Bly learned that patients were often mistreated. Many were dirty and hungry. They were left for long times without care. Instead of getting better, patients got worse.

12   Two weeks later, Bly was out of the asylum. But the outcome of her daring stunt lasted for years. Her reports about asylums were first printed in the *World.* Later, they came out as a book called *Ten Days in a Madhouse.* Readers were shocked by what she wrote. They cried

for changes. Because of Bly, life got better for patients in New York asylums.

The Biggest Trip of All

13   Nellie Bly had proved she was a great reporter. But she still wanted adventure. A book gave her the idea for her greatest success. *Around the World in Eighty Days* was a popular book in 1889. It tells the tale of Phileas [Fil'•ee•us] Fogg, a noted English gentleman. On a bet, he travels around the world in just 80 days. Few people believed the trip was possible. Bly thought she could make the trip even faster.

14   At first, the *World* would not let her try. The idea was crazy. No one could go around the world in so few days! And for a woman, there would be added danger. But Bly kept asking. Finally, her boss told her to go ahead. He knew Bly loved adventure. Besides, the trip could make both her and the paper famous.

15   Bly packed a single bag. Then she set off. On November 14, 1889, at 9:40 A.M., her ship left New Jersey. Bly first landed in England. Then she went on to France. There she met Jules Verne, the writer of *Around the World in Eighty Days*. After Verne wished her good luck, Bly left for Hong Kong.

A Race Against Time

16 Nellie Bly traveled by ship, train, horse, handcart, and burro. Wherever she went, she wrote. She kept an exact record of what she saw and did. Bly planned to share her adventures with others. She wanted her readers to feel as if they had traveled along with her.

17 When Bly's ship from Hong Kong reached San Francisco, she was famous. The *World* sent a train to meet her. It would bring her to New Jersey as fast as it could. Even so, crowds met the train at each stop. Everyone wanted to see the young world traveler.

18 At last, the train reached New Jersey. Bly jumped from it on January 25, 1890, at 3:31 P.M. She had circled Earth in exactly 72 days, 6 hours, and 11 minutes. The waiting crowd cheered. A few days later, New York greeted her. Fireworks went off. Brass bands played. A parade marched down Broadway.

19 Of course, Bly reported on her trip in the *World*. She also wrote *Nellie Bly's Book: Around the World in Seventy-Two Days*. This was her most popular book.

Other Adventures

20 Nellie Bly kept up her writing until 1895. Then she married Robert Seaman, a very rich man.

After he died, she ran his business. But her gift was for news, not business. By 1920, she was writing again.

21   Nellie Bly died in 1922. By then, planes carried people over land and seas. Bly's speed record was broken. Yet Bly's boldness is still a model. And her spirit of adventure will never age.

Questions

1. What was Nellie Bly's real name?

2. What was the first newspaper Bly worked for?

3. What were some topics of Bly's first newspaper reports?

4. What gave Bly the idea for her trip around the world?

5. Why did New York City hold a parade in Bly's honor?

Identifying Character

1. Why was Nellie Bly angry when she read the article in the *Pittsburgh Dispatch?*

2. How and why did Nellie Bly enter the New York insane asylum as a patient? What does that stunt tell you about her?

3. What three words would you use to describe Nellie Bly?

4. Why did Nellie Bly want to travel around the world?

All Kinds of Cats

Why were cats once burned alive?

1 To some people, a cat means beauty and grace. To others, a cat means mystery or power. Cats have held a special place in people's lives for thousands of years.

Traits in Common

2 Except for size, all cats are much the same. All are very strong for their size and move in much the same way. They can be fast and mean. Most can fish. All cats can swim. Some don't really like water unless there is no other way to escape.

3 Most cats can climb. All have good sight, hearing, and smell. All have pads on their feet with sharp claws under them. They kill quickly, so they are great hunters.

An Old Family

4 No one knows when the first cat lived. But the most famous cat of long ago is the saber-toothed tiger. During the Ice Age, this cat moved into all parts of the world. It died out many, many years ago.

5 Cats were part of every family in Egypt 5,000 years ago. They were pets, but they also killed the mice and rats that ate stored grain. People even got their cats to fish and hunt for them. The people of Egypt saw their cats as gods. When a cat died, its owner made it a mummy. In the 1800s, a graveyard just for cats was found in Egypt with mummies of 300,000 cats.

6 People of the Middle Ages were afraid of cats. They believed that cats held the power of black magic. So they began to kill them. They burned them alive in the center of town. Over time, there weren't enough cats left to kill mice and rats. Rat bites made people very sick. Many people died because there were not enough cats.

Close to Home

7 By the 1700s, cats were again friends and mice killers. Today there are about 30 million pet cats in the United States.

8 A little more than 100 years ago, there were no cat breeds. Then people began mating the cats they liked best. A certain color, ear shape, or

leg size was passed down over the years. These became breeds such as Siamese [Sy•uh•meez'], Persian [Per'•zhun], and Manx [Manks]. Clubs around the world help people keep the breeds pure and also start new breeds.

Tigers

9 The biggest wild cat in the world is the tiger. Tigers live in China and other parts of Asia. They are found in no other parts of the world, except in zoos.

10 There are different kinds of tigers, but all have black stripes on a yellow or orange body. The tiger's tail has black rings. A male tiger may weigh as much as 500 pounds and be 10 feet long. Three feet of his length is his tail.

11 Tigers are big, strong, and fierce. They like to hide in the jungle or in thick brush along a river. Tigers can swim better than any other cat. They may walk around during the day to see what's in the area. Then at night they go hunting. Tigers will kill cows, horses, sheep, and goats. They will kill almost any kind of wild animal. But tigers won't go after elephants or bears for fear of getting killed first.

Lions

12 Lions and tigers act much the same. Their bones look alike. They are about the same size.

When a lion and a tiger mate, their offspring is called a liger. Lions and tigers are different in that the lion has no stripes. Also, the male lion has a mane. Most lions stay with their mates for life.

13   Lions also hunt at night, in pairs or groups. The team goes out looking for a zebra, giraffe, or other animal. The female lion hides near a water hole. The male lion scares the animal with his loud roar. The female then jumps on it and bites deeply into its neck. The male keeps up the loud roar. When the animal is dead, he joins the female to feed.

14   Lions and tigers kill people only if they can't go after animals. That can happen if their teeth or claws are broken. It can happen also when they are too old and slow to hunt wild animals.

Other Family Members

15 A leopard may be as long as a lion or tiger. But it has spots and weighs less than 200 pounds. The leopard climbs trees. It jumps long and high. It lives in Asia and Africa.

16   The hunting leopard of India is the cheetah. It can run at speeds of up to 70 miles per hour. That is faster than any other land animal.

17   The jaguar is the leopard's cousin. It is the biggest cat in Central or South America. The

jaguar is six or seven feet long. Not many jaguars are left. They are in danger of dying out.

18   A smaller leopard cousin is the ocelot [ah′•suh•laht]. It weighs 25 to 35 pounds and has both stripes and spots. Some are still found in both the United States and Mexico.

19   Big or small, each kind of cat is important to other living things. The largest tiger helps balance life in the wild. The smallest house cat can brighten the life of a person. Whatever their role, cats are special in our lives and our world.

Questions

1. What was the most famous cat of the Ice Age?

2. How did the people of ancient Egypt feel about cats?

3. What was the effect of burning cats during the Middle Ages?

4. Outside of zoos, where do tigers live?

5. What is a liger?

Comparing and Contrasting/ Identifying Main Idea

1. In what ways are all cats alike?

2. Which cat is the best swimmer?

3. Which cats hunt in pairs or groups?

4. Which cat is the fastest?

5. What is the main idea of this article?

The Great Depression

How did President Franklin Delano Roosevelt make sure that people would have some money for their old age?

1 Today, many of us wish we had more money. But in the 1930s, nearly everyone was in deep money trouble. During the worst times, 14 million people were out of work. Those who did have jobs were paid only pennies. Those terrible years were called the Great Depression.

Trouble Brewing

2 The trouble started in the 1920s. Most of those years, everything seemed to be fine. But things were not as good as they seemed. Farmers were not getting fair prices for crops. Coal mining, railroad, and clothing businesses were having a hard time. And too many people were getting bank loans they could not pay off.

3   Then, in 1929, prices of stock in American business began to drop. A stock once worth $100 might end up being worth only $3. On October 29, 1929, the stock market "crashed" to an all-time low. It was called Black Tuesday. Anyone who owned stocks lost a great deal of money. Suddenly, many rich people were poor.

Hard Times

4 That was the start of the Great Depression. Many companies went out of business. Millions of workers lost their jobs. When people went to get their money, they found the banks were closed. There was no welfare, unemployment checks, or social security. Millions of people went broke. The same thing was happening in other countries, too.

From Bad to Worse

5 President Herbert Hoover promised that better times were "just around the corner." He didn't think the government should step in. But over the next three years, wages fell for those who still had jobs. Prices also fell, but low prices didn't help. Most people were lucky to pay for food and rent. Some families ate "cracker soup" for dinner. Others sorted through garbage for food.

6   Many families lost their homes. They built shacks out of boxes, tin, and old car parts. They

slept under newspapers. Soup kitchens and bread lines were set up. Some children stopped going to school because they didn't have clothes to wear. Men out of work stood on the street selling apples for five cents. Others begged in the street. Many people who had lost hope killed themselves.

7 The weather made matters even worse. In 1930, there was little rain. The land from South Dakota to Texas to Illinois—called the Dust Bowl—became as dry as sand. Then, in 1931 and 1932, dust storms blew whole farms away. Sand got into food and water. People stayed indoors. They stuffed cloth and paper into any holes in their houses so the wind could not get in.

8 A few years later, there was too much rain. Eleven large rivers flooded. In Ohio, 500,000 homes were washed away. Towns along the great rivers were washed out.

The New Deal

9 Herbert Hoover ran for president again in 1932. But he lost to Franklin Delano Roosevelt. President Roosevelt believed that the government should step in to end the depression. His plan was called the New Deal. It started a number of new programs.

10 Roosevelt and Congress put new government controls on banks and the stock

market. They sent out $500 million to help the poorest people. They set up jobs for people to plant trees and build dams and power plants. To drive up farm prices, they paid farmers to plant less. To help people keep their homes and farms, they gave government loans. They worked with companies to hire more workers.

More Programs

11 Then the Works Progress Administration, or WPA, began. Under this new program, people built schools, hospitals, bridges, roads, airports, and government buildings. It also paid people to paint, sculpt, write, dance, and make music. Even today, many post offices, schools, and parks have works by WPA artists.

12 In 1935, Social Security began. Workers paid a tax so they would have money in their old age. Social Security paid women and children who had lost a working man in the family. It also started a state welfare program and an unemployment plan. People who were out of work would get some money until they found another job.

13 President Roosevelt helped the country make it through the Great Depression. Not everyone liked what he did. Yet Roosevelt was the only president to win the office of president four times.

Chasing Away the Blues

14 Movies filled with music and dance helped people to smile through the worst of the 1930s. Hollywood came into its own and radio became a big hit. People heard Bing Crosby sing. They enjoyed listening to radio shows such as "The Shadow" and "The Lone Ranger." They laughed with Bob Hope or listened to new music by Benny Goodman, the "King of Swing." But the most famous song of the depression was "Brother, Can You Spare a Dime?"

Coming Back

15 Slowly, America crawled out of the Great Depression. But Roosevelt's programs alone could not end this awful time. When World War II broke out, America needed its factories and farms again. Men went off to fight, while women went to work. The war got America back on its feet.

16 The country has been up and down since the Great Depression. But the laws passed under Roosevelt helped make sure that it can never happen again.

Questions

1. What year did the stock market crash?

2. Who was the president at the time?

3. What was the New Deal?

4. What is Social Security, and when did it start?

5. How many times did Roosevelt win the presidency?

Identifying Cause and Effect/Drawing Conclusions

1. What were some of the causes of the Great Depression?

2. What were some of the effects of the Great Depression?

3. Why were parts of the United States called the Dust Bowl in 1930s?

4. Why was Herbert Hoover defeated by Franklin Roosevelt in the 1932 presidential election?

5. Besides the New Deal, what helped end the Great Depression? How?

Electric Cars

Are you getting choked up over gas fumes? Perhaps it's time for another kind of car.

1 Try to think of life without cars. It's not easy. But our cars make us sick. Their exhaust pollutes the air. Dirty air is hard to breathe. On some days in large cities, the air is thick and gray. Polluted air drifts all over. It even rises high above Earth. Many scientists feel that it can change the weather. Everyone is hurt by pollution.

2 Each day there are more cars, buses, and trucks. Each day they cause more pollution. We can't get rid of our vehicles. But we can change them. Their gasoline engines are the problem. Vehicles could be powered some other way. A likely form of energy is electricity. Today, researchers are trying to build a useful electric car.

3   The electric car is not a new idea. The first electrics were made about 100 years ago. In fact, three kinds of engines were used on early cars.

Early Electrics

4   Around 1900, thousands of cars ran on electric batteries. They were silent, so they never scared horses. They were clean. They were easy to start. Almost every woman driver chose an electric car.

5   But electric cars were slow. Their top speed was 20 or 30 miles per hour. Going uphill, top speed fell to 4 or 5 miles per hour. Even worse, they couldn't go far. After about 30 miles, the batteries had to be recharged.

Some Progress

6   Other cars had steam engines. A steam-powered car was almost as clean as an electric. And it was much faster. Racing steamers reached speeds of over 100 miles per hour. With normal use, steamers ran at 30 miles per hour for more than 150 miles.

7   Cars with gasoline engines also went fast. And they had a wider range. Refueling took only minutes. As long as a car could get fuel, its range had almost no limits.

8   But these gasoline-powered cars had drawbacks. There were many moving parts

that could break. They often did. A driver had to fix many things on, in, and under the car. Driving one of these cars could be dirty. Worst of all, the engine had to be cranked before the car would start. Only a strong person could do that.

9   Then, in 1912, the self-starter came into use. Now an electric battery, not a crank, would start a gas-powered car. Suddenly, these cars were as easy to start as electrics. They were already as fast as steamers. Both the electric car and the steamer began to lose ground. Within 20 years, no one made them anymore.

Modern Electrics

10 In the 1960s, attention turned once more to the electric car. What could increase its speed and range?

11   Some researchers looked at the lead-acid battery. They tried new designs. They tried different materials. Some batteries they made were better than those of today. But the strongest ones cost too much.

12   Other researchers worked on a slightly different power source. It is called a fuel cell. A fuel cell could be twice as strong as a lead-acid battery. But, even today, it is too heavy and costly.

13   Recharging was also studied. Drivers wouldn't mind stopping so often for a recharging if it took only minutes. Still another idea was to design a lighter car. Then a regular battery could push it faster and farther.

14   Today, many designs are being tested. Large and small companies and even people on their own are building electrics. Reports say that work is moving ahead.

Road Tests

15   One owner tried to drive cross-country in his modern electric car in 1991. Noel Perrin later wrote about his trip in *Solo: Life with an Electric Car.* Perrin was happy with his car's speed on flat land. The car could go 50 miles per hour easily. It went up to 60 miles between charges. For short bursts, the car could even reach 60 miles per hour.

16   But going up a steep hill, the car could barely reach 30 miles per hour. Worse, it ran out of power very quickly.

17   Each time Perrin stopped to recharge, he had big problems. There were no charging stations along the highways. So Perrin had to plug his car into regular outlets. At best, recharging took four hours. Sometimes it took

twice that time. That meant that Perrin could travel only about 100 miles a day.

18   The same year, someone else drove an electric car for 24 hours straight under special conditions. Recharging was much quicker. This car went more than 600 miles.

19   In 1992, an electric vehicle did even better with a new charging station. A small electric truck was driven around a race track. Every 60 miles or so, it pulled into the station. A computer controlled the recharging. Each time, the job took less than 20 minutes. The truck traveled 831.8 miles in 24 hours, a new world record.

Planning Ahead

20 Could we have fast charging stations—or electricity pumps—along the roads? These would give electric cars the range they need. But such pumps would cause new problems.

21   Electric power companies have more than enough energy at night. Electric cars that are recharged at night could use that energy. But suppose that they needed to recharge during the day. Then they would need to stop at electricity pumps. The power companies would have to put out more energy. So the power companies would do more polluting,

since coal is used to make electricity. That wouldn't help.

22   In short, there is little chance that your next car will be an electric. But each step takes researchers a little further. Why not plan ahead? It may be time to start an electric car savings fund.

Questions

1. About what year did cars first run on electric batteries?

2. How fast could the first electrics go?

3. What new addition to gas-powered cars made them more popular than electric- or steam-powered cars?

4. Name two things that made Noel Perrin unhappy with his electric car.

5. What was the 1992 world record for distance traveled in 24 hours?

Making Predictions

1. Predict what your life would be like without a car. What changes would you have to make? Would your life be easier or more difficult?

2. Imagine that electric cars become popular. Predict how fueling stations would operate. Would people have to use less electricity elsewhere to have enough for their cars? Would the cost of electricity increase or decrease?

3. In the near future, widespread use of electric cars seems unlikely. What do you think will happen if gas-powered cars continue to be used? Write a letter to the editor predicting the effect on the environment and offer a solution.

Pride of the Giants

Why did Chief Meyers quit his studies— all expenses paid—at one of the best schools in the country?

1 John "Chief" Meyers was a major league baseball player about 90 years ago. He was proud to be in baseball. He was just as proud of his Native American heritage.

2   The Cahuillas [Kah•hoo•ee'•yuz] were one of the tribes of the Mission Indians of southern California. They lived high in the peaks of the San Jacinto [Juh•seen'•toe] Mountains. John Tortes Meyers was born in a Cahuilla village in 1880. His people were known as a proud and independent tribe. It is no wonder that Mcyers grew up to be that way, too.

Following a Dream

3 When Meyers was about 11, the family moved to the city of Riverside. He attended public schools there. When he finished high school, college was far from his mind. His heart was set on playing baseball.

4 Meyers's skills were so good that several semiprofessional [seh•mi•proh•feh′•shun•ul] teams hired him as a catcher. Meyers made no secret of his Native American background. He was aware of the prejudice against minorities in those days. But he had pride in his heritage. Soon he got the nickname of "Chief."

Help from Abroad

5 In 1904, Chief Meyers's life took an interesting turn. His baseball team was playing in Albuquerque [Al′•buh•ker•kee], New Mexico. That's where he met an all-American football player named Ralph Glaze. Glaze was a student at Dartmouth College in New Hampshire.

6 Glaze told Meyers about a scholarship at Dartmouth. Who had set up the scholarship? An earl in England! In the 1700s, the school was known as Moor's Indian Charity School. The teachers were English missionaries [mih′•shun•air•eez]. The earl of Dartmouth heard about the school. He sent money for a

special scholarship fund. The scholarship could go only to a Native American who was a good enough student to study there. The school was later renamed for the earl.

7   Meyers put in for the scholarship and was accepted. He could not play baseball for the school because he was not an amateur [am'•uh•cher]. When school was out for the summer, he played for Harrisburg, Pennsylvania, in the Tri-State League. He had planned to return to Dartmouth at the end of the summer. But he was called home to the bedside of his sick mother. When her health improved, it was too late for him to return to school. He regretted that for the rest of his life.

Play Ball

8   The best thing Chief Meyers could pursue was another career in baseball. At first, he played for minor league teams in Montana and Minnesota. In 1908, he joined the National League's New York Giants.

9   At that time, John McGraw was the team's manager. Meyers greatly admired him. He felt that McGraw had changed the public's feeling toward baseball players. In the early part of the century, players were not always treated with respect. As an example, they weren't allowed in the better hotels for out-of-town games. But

McGraw didn't go along with that. He paid for his players to stay at the best hotels.

Hail to the Chief

10 Chief Meyers also had great respect for umpire Bill Klem and Giants pitcher Christy Mathewson. By 1910, Meyers became the team's regular catcher. His highest batting average was .358 in 1912. The team won pennants in 1911, 1912, and 1913.

11   In 1916, Meyers was traded to the Brooklyn Robins (later renamed the Dodgers). Meyers retired the following year. His lifetime batting average was .291. His top salary was about $6,000 a year.

It's All in the Game

12 The subject of salary came up in an interview when Chief Meyers was in his 80s. Meyers said that today's players are businessmen. "They've got agents and outside interests and all that sort of thing. We played for money, too. Naturally. That's how we made our living. But mostly we played just for the love of it. . . . Most of us would have paid *them* just to let us play. We loved baseball."

13   In that same interview, Meyers compared himself to an old warrior chief of the great Six Nations. The chief had said, "I am like an old

hemlock. My head is still high, but the winds of close to 100 winters have whistled through my branches, and I have been witness to many wondrous and many tragic things. My eyes perceive the present, but my roots are imbedded deeply in the grandeur of the past." Chief Meyers died in 1971 at the age of 90.

Questions

1. Where does the Cahuilla tribe come from?

2. Why was John Meyers nicknamed "Chief"?

3. What year did Meyers join the New York Giants?

4. Why did Meyers admire the Giants' manager, John McGraw?

5. What position did Meyers play most often with the Giants?

Fact vs. Opinion

1. Do you think that the nickname "Chief" showed respect or disrespect for John Meyers? Why?

2. Do you think professional athletes are overpaid today? Write a paragraph defending your opinion.

3. "John 'Chief' Meyers was a credit to the game of baseball." Use facts from the article to support this opinion.

Life Beneath a Blanket of Snow

How does snow act as a blanket for animals?

1 Flake by flake, snow covers the ground in winter in cold areas. This blanket can last for weeks or months. It's hard for rabbits, birds, and deer to find food in the snow. But other animals need the snow to protect them.

2 Fresh snow looks smooth and clean. Underneath, the ground is the same as it was in the fall. There are fallen trees and leaves on the forest floor. There are rock piles under the cliffs and tall grass in the fields. Short grass covers the lawns. When snow falls, it does not fill in every space. It bends the grass. It flows around trees and rocks. It isn't a solid block. Under it are spaces and tunnels.

3   Under the snow, it is warmer and brighter than you might think. In summer, the sun warms the soil, which stores up this heat. In winter, the heat rises toward the cold air. If there were no snow, all the heat would escape. The ground would be frozen solid. But snow acts as a blanket. It keeps the ground much warmer than the temperature that we feel in the air.

Animals Under the Snow

4 Some animals, like the fox, may dig into the snow to make a warm shelter from a storm. But many small animals live under the snow all winter long.

5   The largest of these animals is the red squirrel. It is about one foot long and weighs less than seven ounces. Most of the year, red squirrels live in trees. But when it gets cold, red squirrels build tunnels under the snow. They eat pine cones they have stored during the fall.

6   Meadow voles [volz], which are like mice, need snow to stay alive. Most of the year they live in burrows under the surface of the ground. When it is freezing cold and there is no snow on the ground, meadow voles are in danger. The ground begins to freeze. Their burrows can't protect them from the weather.

7   Once it snows, life becomes easier for meadow voles. The snow blanket keeps the ground warm. And the bottom layer of snow becomes loose and easy to tunnel through. Meadow voles build nests under the snow.

8   Because they are small, meadow voles must eat often to keep up their body heat. They dig tunnels near their nests and eat all the plants they find on the way. When the snow melts, you can tell where their tunnels were. There are narrow trails of very short grass.

Sharing Warmth

9 Meadow voles have many relatives. Some of these are prairie voles, pine voles, deer mice, and shrews. In warm weather, these animals keep to themselves. But in winter, they share their nests with others of their kind. Sleeping together keeps all the animals warmer. The animals take turns leaving the nest to feed. This way, the nest is always warm when they return.

10   There are drawbacks to these shared nests. It is easy for sickness to spread from one animal to another. And predators [pred'•uh•torz] are more likely to find the nests because of their strong smell.

The Hunters

11 There are many predators of these small animals. They include foxes, coyotes, owls, hawks, weasels, and house cats. These predators may hear or smell a vole moving under the snow. But they will have a hard time catching one.

12 The long, thin weasel [wee'•zul] is the best hunter. It can easily dig through snow and travel along tunnels. Often a weasel will take over a nest. It will eat the animals inside and line the walls with their fur. When the snow melts, you can see these fur-lined nests. They tell the tale of life and death under the snow.

13 Shrews also hunt under the snow. They are not good diggers, so they use tunnels made by other animals. Shrews need a lot of food, so they hunt for insects. Shrews sniff to find their prey. They also use their whiskers to feel prey and their ears to hear it moving.

Insect and Plants

14 Snow fleas are closely tied to winter. They are found in the northeastern part of the United States. These little blue insects live in the leaves on the forest floor. On warm days, they come to the surface of the snow. There may be enough of them to form a dark patch on the snow.

15   Snow fleas are also known as springtails because they can jump. When the temperature drops, they go back under the snow. Snow fleas are proof of life under the snow.

16   Plants get a head start on spring under the snow. Light can get through the snow and make the ground warm and moist. This lets plants live and grow. Some plants, like wild onions, push through the snow. Other plants, like snow buttercups or glacier [glay'•sher] lilies, even bloom above the snow.

17   As spring arrives, the snow melts. The plants and animals that live safely under the snow must get ready for the new season. There will be many challenges ahead. But when winter returns, the snow will again provide a blanket to protect them.

Questions

1. Which is the largest animal that lives under the snow?

2. Why do meadow voles eat often?

3. What are some drawbacks of shared nests?

4. Which animal is the best hunter of animals that live under the snow?

5. How do shrews find their prey?

6. Why are springtails a good name for snow fleas?

Applying Passage Elements

1. Why isn't the ground frozen solid in the winter?

2. How does sharing a nest below ground help meadow voles and their relatives?

3. How does light help plants under the snow?

Answer Key

A Home in the North
Page 9: Questions
1. A snow house could be built in an hour or two.
2. *Eskimo* means "a person who eats raw meat."
3. Today people in the Arctic live in modern frame homes, use snowmobiles, and have indoor jobs.

Page 9: Antonym/Synonym Search
1. Possible answers: hot–cold; slower–faster; small–big; summer–winter; wet–dry; long–short; soft–hard; thin–fat; down–up; slowly–quickly
2. A hole was cut in the roof of the snow house to let the stale air out. Fresh air would come in through the tunnel.
3. Answers will vary.
4. Possible answers: weary–tired; start–begin; enormous–huge; arched–curved; fast–quick; uncooked–raw
5. Answers will vary.

What Is Color?
Page 13: Questions
1. A prism works by bending a ray of light and spreading out the colors.
2. Light hits the colors of an object. Some of this light is reflected off the object and into our eyes.
3. Cones respond to color.
4. The cones in our eyes do not work in dim light.

Page 13: Using Context Clues
1. Red, yellow, and blue are primary colors.
2. Complementary colors are opposites. Yellow is complementary to blue. Blue green is complementary to red.
3. An afterimage is an image with the same shape as an original image, but with different colors.

Who Wears the Pants?
Page 18: Questions
1. Men started wearing pants to ride horses easier and to keep warm.
2. Women started wearing pants by 1890 to make riding bicycles and playing sports easier.
3. It was hard for women to buy stockings during the war, so they wore pants to cover their bare legs.
4. Plaid is a pattern that has colored stripes going in two different directions.
5. Men in Scotland wear kilts to show which part of Scotland they come from.

Page 18: Spelling Word Alert
1. piece–peace; sew–so; wear–where; great–grate; bare–bear; sense–cents; two–too
2. *Knee* has a silent letter (k) and names a part of the body. Before you give a gift, you *wrap* it; *wrap* has a silent letter (w).
3. Lines 6–7: That way, everyone could *admire* their good-looking legs. *admiring*

Lines 7–9: The men would look in the mirror to *decide* which of their legs was better looking. *deciding*

Egypt's Wonders

Page 24: Questions
1. Each pyramid was built as a tomb.
2. Farmers worked from July to November while their fields were flooded from the Nile River.
3. The king's body was preserved so his soul could live forever.
4. People wanted to enter the tombs to steal gold and jewels that were entombed with the mummies.

Page 24: Noting Details
1. King Khufu's pyramid is 481 feet high.
2. King Khufu's pyramid is also called the Great Pyramid.
3. The workers built a ramp of stones and mud to get blocks up to each layer of the pyramid.
4. The pyramid had more than 120 layers.
5. The walls of the secret rooms had beautiful pictures and writings that told about the king's life.
6. The king's body was wrapped in layers of cloth.

A Good Cup of Coffee

Page 29: Questions
1. The best coffee trees are in South America and Africa.
2. Coffee berries ripen in 6 to 14 months.
3. Coffee beans are treated with a chemical and then the caffeine is steamed out.
4. A young French soldier brought one coffee tree with him on a sailing ship around 1700.

Page 29: Identifying Sequence
1. After coffee berries are picked, they are spread out in the sun to dry.
2. Coffee berries are roasted after they are shipped to other countries.
3. Before coffee is shipped to stores, it is packed in air tight containers.

The Trail of Tears

Page 35: Questions
1. The Cherokee's original home was the Great Smoky Mountains in Tennessee.
2. Andrew Jackson was president at the time of the march.
3. The Cherokees faced a lack of warm clothes and shoes, bad weather, disease, and hunger.
4. Those who died were thrown into ditches dug along the trail.
5. It took about six months to march to Oaklahoma.

Page 35: Recognizing Stated Concepts
1. White men wanted the gold and the Cherokees had to give up their land.
2. The U.S. government told the Cherokees that they had to relocate to the Oaklahoma Territory.
3. The Cherokees had only the food they could carry; their

grain sacks would get wet and would soon be filled with bugs.

Ellis Island

Page 41: Questions

1. More than 100 million Americans have ancestors who came through Ellis Island.
2. People came to the U.S. to find work, to avoid army service in their home country, and to avoid unfair treatment at home.
3. The immigrants' greatest fear was the health station on Ellis Island.
4. Today Ellis Island is a museum and memorial.

Page 41: Signs and Map Skills

1–3 Answers will vary.

Building a Budget

Page 46: Questions

1. A budget helps you keep track of your money.
2. Income and expenses are the two main parts of a budget.
3. Income is money you earn. Net income is the amount of money you actually get after taxes and insurance are deducted.
4. To figure out how much you spend each month, you could make a list, save receipts, and keep track of expenses.

Page 46: Making Graphs

1–2 Answers will vary.

Armchair Shopping

Page 53: Questions

1. "Junk mail" holds holds no interest for them.

2. If you buy through the mail, you can shop from home and you have a wider variety of choices.
3. If you buy through the mail, you can't inspect what you are buying, you have to pay shipping costs, and you have to wait for what you buy.
4. If you use a credit card and something goes wrong with the order, it is easy to cancel your debt.
5. You can stop junk mail by writing to the Direct Marketing Association to ask them to remove your name from their list.

Page 53: Using Consumer Materials

1. COD–cash on delivery; F.O.B.–freight on board; H/C–handling charge; est.–estimate; min.–minimum; lbs.–pounds; item no.–item number; qty.–quantity; exp. date–expiration date
2–3 Answers will vary.

The Fabulous Miss Bly

Page 60: Questions

1. Nellie Bly's real name was Elizabeth Cochrane.
2. *Pittsburgh Dispatch* was the first newspaper she worked for.
3. Bly reported on working women, slums, and divorce.
4. Bly's idea for the trip around the world came from the book *Around the World in Eighty Days*.
5. New York held a parade because Bly made the trip around the world in record time.

Page 60: Identifying Character
1. Bly felt that women could do many jobs well outside the home.
2. Bly entered the insane asylum to report on the conditions of an asylum. She pretended that she was insane. This showed that Bly was a brave and caring person.
3. Answers will vary.
4. Bly wanted to travel around the world because she loved adventure and wanted to make her paper and herself famous.

All Kinds of Cats

Page 66: Questions
1. The saber-toothed tiger was the most famous cat of the Ice Age.
2. The people of ancient Egypt loved and honored their cats like gods.
3. During the Middle Ages, the lack of cats available to kill rats and mice led to the plague that killed millions of people.
4. Tigers live in China and other parts of Asia.
5. A liger is a cross between a lion and a tiger.

Page 66: Comparing and Contrasting/Identifying Main Idea
1. Answers will vary.
2. The tiger is the best swimmer.
3. Lions hunt in groups or pairs.
4. The cheetah is the fastest cat.
5. There are many different kinds of cats in our world.

The Great Depression

Page 72: Questions
1. The stock market crashed in 1929.
2. Herbert Hoover was president during the Great Depression.
3. The New Deal was a plan to help end the depression.
4. Social Security started in 1935. It provides benefits and payments to people when they retire.
5. Roosevelt won the presidency four times.

Page 72: Identifying Cause and Effect/Drawing Conclusions
1. Causes of the Great Depression: farmers were not getting fair prices; mining, railroads, and businesses were having a hard time; too many people were getting bank loans they could not pay off; stock prices dropped.
2. Effects of the Great Depression: rich people became poor; companies went out of business; workers lost their jobs; banks closed; people went broke, lost their homes, and didn't have enough to eat.
3. Some parts of the U.S. were called the Dust Bowl because there was little rain that year.
4. Roosevelt defeated Hoover in 1932 because Hoover didn't feel that the government should take over and end the depression and Roosevelt did.
5. Besides the New Deal, the WPA and Social Security helped end the Great Depression. Answers will vary.

Electric Cars

Page 78: Questions
1. Cars ran on electric batteries around 1900.
2. The first electric cars could go 20 or 30 miles per hour.
3. The self-starter made gas-powered cars more popular.
4. Noel Perrin's car could barely reach 30 miles per hour going up a hill, and it ran out of power quickly.
5. The 1992 world record was 831.8 miles in 24 hours.

Page 79: Making Predictions
1–3 Answers will vary.

Pride of the Giants

Page 85: Questions
1. The Cahuilla tribe came from southern California.
2. John Meyers was called "Chief" because of his Native American background.
3. Meyers joined the New York Giants in 1908.
4. McGraw changed the public's feelings toward baseball players and also treated his players with respect.
5. Meyers was usually the Giants' catcher.

Page 85: Fact vs. Opinion
1–3 Answers will vary.

Life Beneath a Blanket of Snow

Page 91: Questions
1. The largest animal living under the snow is the red squirrel.
2. Meadow voles must eat often to keep up their body heat.
3. Because of shared nests, sickness can spread from one animal to another and predators can find the nest easier because of the strong smell.
4. The best hunter under the snow is the weasel.
5. Shrews sniff and use their whiskers and ears to find their prey.
6. Snow fleas are called springtails because they can jump.

Page 91: Applying Passage Elements
1. Snow acts as a blanket to keep the ground warm during the winter.
2. Meadow voles and their relatives keep each other warm when sleeping. They keep the nest warm when the animals take turns leaving the nest to feed.
3. Light can get through the snow and make the ground warm and moist. This lets plants live and grow.